Politics & Mission

*Rediscovering the Political Power
of What Christians Do*

— MARTIN GAINSBOROUGH —

Sacristy
Press

Sacristy Press
PO Box 612, Durham, DH1 9HT

www.sacristy.co.uk

First published in 2023 by Sacristy Press, Durham

Bible extracts, unless otherwise stated, are from the *New
Revised Standard Version Bible: Anglicized Edition*, copyright
1989, 1995, Division of Christian Education of the National
Council of the Churches of Christ in the United States
of America. Used by permission. All rights reserved.

Extracts from Common Worship: Services and
Prayers for the Church of England are © Archbishops'
Council 2005. Published by Church House Publishing.
Used by permission. rights@hymnsam.co.uk

Every reasonable effort has been made to trace the
copyright holders of material reproduced in this
book, but if any have been inadvertently overlooked
the publisher would be glad to hear from them.

Sacristy Limited, registered in England
& Wales, number 7565667

British Library Cataloguing-in-Publication Data
A catalogue record for the book is available
from the British Library

ISBN 978-1-78959-270-2

Contents

Foreword iv
Acknowledgements. viii
Introduction. 1

Chapter 1. Political liberalism 7
Chapter 2. Liturgy revisited 17
Chapter 3. Morning Prayer. 29
Chapter 4. Baptism. 37
Chapter 5. Eucharist. 49
Chapter 6. Footwashing 63
Chapter 7. Funeral 75

Conclusion. 93

Foreword

At the State Funeral of Her Majesty the Queen on 19 September 2022, there were two booklets on each seat in Westminster Abbey. The first was the *Ceremonial* which set out the timings that would determine just how a long and brilliantly imagined day would unfold. The *Ceremonial* told us the way in which processions should assemble. There were directions for His Majesty's Body Guard of the Honourable Corps of Gentlemen at Arms, the Lady Usher of the Black Rod, Pursuivants, Heralds and Kings of Arms, the Royal Family and many more. Here was the pattern and performance of state. It was a nation arranged and put in order. It was a conscious display of a set of assumptions about sovereignty.

The second booklet was the *Order of Service* for the Funeral. It was every bit as carefully conceived, and it was the equal of all the panoply of state we saw outside on the streets. The assumptions in the Abbey, however, were of a different order and the language was electric. Conversation about the Late Queen, before the Funeral, had been full of affection and admiration. So much was said over so many days that it is startling to note that significant things had been left unsaid. Just days before the Funeral, I talked to the Cardinal Archbishop of Westminster, and we commented on the silences that fell during national mourning. The silence of those who walked past the coffin in Westminster Hall, the silence of all those mute bunches of flowers left in the royal parks. The silence with which we confront death.

Not in Westminster Abbey. It was a note that appeared in no ceremonial, not printed, not widely shared, but the clergy knew it, so did the choir and so indeed did the bearer party and the College of Heralds. We faced west to meet the coffin as it arrived at the Great West Door. We always knew we would have to turn to begin the procession towards the choir. Our instruction was simple. We listened for the opening words of the service, William Croft's *Funeral Sentences* sung by the Choir: "I am the resurrection and the life, saith the Lord." We turned, together, at the word *resurrection*. The liturgy altered the direction of travel and gave us a new language. We stepped out in hope. The Abbey crackled with a form of theological static.

Those listening carefully will have noticed other moments when, in worship, we found a register we had previously lacked. We spoke confidently and honestly of a life and death we all share. We spoke of hope and resurrection. We also acknowledged a common humanity. The day ended with Garter King of Arms reading out the titles of the Queen as her coffin descended into the royal vault:

> ... the late Most High, Most Mighty, and Most
> Excellent Monarch, Elizabeth the Second, by
> the Grace of God of the United Kingdom of
> Great Britain and Northern Ireland and of Her
> other Realms and Territories Queen, Head of
> the Commonwealth, Defender of the Faith, and
> Sovereign of the Most Noble Order of the Garter.

In the Abbey, however, in the Funeral, we told a story, rooted in faith, in which she has a place, and so do we. Our Late Majesty now became our "sister":

> ... we may rest in him, as our hope is this our
> sister doth.

Reflecting on that day in the weeks that have followed, I was quickly conscious that we had done something of significance in the Abbey: not just performed the proper ceremonial, but spoken deep truths and witnessed to a faith that holds us in community, gives us common cause and frames our greater destiny. Reading this book, I am better able to name the truly "political" significance of the day. Reporting on the Funeral, one newspaper observed:

> Rarely has one place felt so filled with status and
> so empty of malice as Westminster Abbey did
> on Monday.[*]

---

[*] *Financial Times*, 20 September 2022, p. 3.

It is a depressing fact of life in modern Westminster that Parliament Square does not often feel "empty of malice". The liberal project fails all around us as we abandon assumptions about how we manage our common life, or even deny that there can be such a thing. As Martin explains, the subversive gospel keeps insisting that we can hope for more than a means for managing disagreement—it insists on common cause and a shared experience. We are a people who are fashioned by our dependency on grace and who can find resilience and a fresh honesty in faith. We can and will speak of our humanity, of life and death, and of our shared hope.

The Very Revd Dr David Hoyle MBE, FSA
Dean of Westminster

Acknowledgements

The debts incurred in any piece of writing are always substantial and not easily mapped. However, I am acutely conscious of a series of writers whose texts have surrounded me, stimulated and challenged me, over many years. Among those whose writing has been most formative the following stand out: Malcolm Brown, William Cavanaugh, Elaine Graham, Stanley Hauerwas, John Milbank, Adrian Pabst, Anna Rowlands, Sam Wells and Rowan Williams. Beyond this, I am grateful to the communities I have been part of: St Luke's Barton Hill in East Bristol; the School of Sociology, Politics and International Studies in the University of Bristol; Bristol Cathedral; the Bishop of Bristol's Office; and the Bishop of Bristol's Staff Team. At Bristol Cathedral, I am grateful to two Deans, the Very Revd Dr David Hoyle, now Dean of Westminster, who has kindly written the book's foreword, and the Very Revd Dr Mandy Ford. Bristol Cathedral has long been a special place for me where I have prayed and worshipped and felt appreciated and affirmed. I would particularly like to express my gratitude to Bristol Cathedral's Social Justice Group and the

Homeless Outreach Team, whose company and support I have valued hugely, and who have been exemplars of faithful Christian witness. Delydd McAdam, a member of both groups, read and commented on a draft of the manuscript, and for that I am grateful. I have Larraine Clark, also a member of the Cathedral community, to thank for the concluding paragraph of Chapter 6. I would like to thank my colleagues in the Bishop of Bristol's Office, Sarah Beach and Anita Van Wyk, who never complained when I "paused" administrative duties to do some writing, and especially to the Bishop of Bristol, the Rt Revd Vivienne Faull, from whom I have learnt so much, not least about liturgy. Grateful thanks also go to my editor at Sacristy Press, Dr Natalie Watson, and all those who have worked on the book, and to Hymns Ancient & Modern for permission to quote from *Common Worship*. Finally, I would like to thank my family, who have been there for me through thick and thin, and especially my firstborn, Annie Gainsborough, who was the first to read and comment on each chapter and whose gentle wisdom, insight and encouragement I have so appreciated. I have written this book to try and say something that might be heard beyond the academy, particularly by lay Christians sitting in the pews. I hope and pray that it *will* be heard and that together we may grow in confidence in God's mission.

Martin Gainsborough
1 October 2022

Introduction

Jesus taught us to call God our Father,
and so with confidence we pray.
Introduction to the Lord's Prayer

When I was at Bristol Cathedral, I helped start a homeless outreach project, connecting with people sleeping on the streets, offering kindness, prayer, conversation and a hot drink. Thanks to the devotion and commitment of the team, the work has continued long after I have moved on. It is demanding work. People's needs are complex and often overwhelming. Getting help—particularly interfacing with a bureaucratic system—is not easy. It is hard, in the circumstances, to maintain one's morale when months go by and little seems to change, and you feel powerless to help. Thus, for the Christian, there are some important but hard lessons to learn about not being able to fix things. Yet the work always felt of profound importance—quietly and without fanfare Jesus' love was shown, someone's day was brightened, and—perhaps more unexpectedly—those of us who took part in the outreach were changed by the encounter.

Up and down the land, we all have our own stories to tell of the quiet, sacrificial work that the Church does so well—making a practical difference, bringing hope and the love of Jesus to those who are in need.

These are the stories we like to tell, and rightly so. It is the Church at its very best.

And yet there is another story, which for the sake of God's mission also needs to be told, though it is perhaps more painful—harder to bear—especially for those of us who are invested in the institution, where the pressure to keep the narrative positive is strong.

Yes, there are amazing stories of faith and hope and new life—thanks be to God!

But it also true that many in our churches feel a bit beleaguered, a bit overdone.

As the years go by, it has become harder and harder to keep the show on the road. Numbers are down. Financial giving is down. Congregations are older, and we wonder if we will still be here in a generation or two.

More than this, in the Church we can sometimes feel unloved. It is as if the nation has fallen out of love with us. People have better things to do on a Sunday, and we are not widely seen as a happening place or a place at the cutting edge. Granted that the Church sometimes doesn't help itself with its failings and squabbles, but none of this is easy to bear, and we can lose confidence.

Our response as Church to this state of affairs typically takes a number of forms. We proclaim the gospel ever more loudly. We go into overdrive with initiatives.

We turn inwards, not worrying too much about "the world" as long as "our people" turn up. This is church as a private members' club. But all this, one suspects, displays a lack of confidence, a fearfulness, rather than a *confidence* in the power of the gospel.

And yet, how deeply ironic this is!

Christianity is electric, fresh, relevant, contemporary and radical!

Christianity is also profoundly political—though not necessarily in the way people conventionally think of politics. But we have lost confidence here too, succumbing either to the secular narrative that the Church should "stay out of politics" or jumping on every contemporary bandwagon such that the Church lacks authenticity, and it is unclear what we bring distinctively as compared with any other political movement. Neither position is right.

And what we absolutely never do is view the Church's liturgy, the words we use in worship, as political. That is, we do not see how our liturgies speak powerfully and directly against the dominant political culture of our day, which is itself creaking at the seams pointing to the need for a major political reset and a rediscovery of what truly matters and what will bring us together.[*]

What an opportunity for the Church and those who share our concerns! And yet, do we—does the Church— seize this opportunity?

---

[*] Adrian Pabst, *The Demons of Liberal Democracy* (Cambridge and Medford, MA: Polity Press, 2019).

There are two inter-related issues here: first, neither Christians nor others are generally well versed in the political ideas that shape society (i.e. we are not able to articulate what they are); and second, we don't see how Christianity says something radically and refreshingly different in comparison (because we are not clear about the political ideas we live by!). Radical and fresh in relation to what, one might ask.

Put differently, we go to church (those of us who do). We hear the words; we see the gestures and the movement, but we don't really hear what's being said. Thus, in the face of our detractors, who think we are dull and out of touch, we are not really able to correct them. In fact, we might even agree! Irony indeed.

This book aims to address these issues. It is ultimately a book about mission, but one that starts in an unusual place. To strengthen mission, the book argues, we need a short lesson in political theory. Then we will be able to see how, through our liturgy, the Church says something radically different from the political ideas which predominate. The hope is that after reading this book your experience of the liturgy, your sense of how the Church is political, and your confidence as a disciple will be strengthened and transformed.*

---

*   For the purposes of the book, the Church is understood as a "space cleared by God through Jesus where we can see properly (God, God's creation, ourselves) and in which people may become what God made them to be". See Rowan Williams, "The Christian Priest Today", lecture on the occasion of the 150th anniversary of Ripon College, Cuddesdon, 28 May 2004. <http://rowanwilliams.archbishopofcanterbury.org/

The book doesn't believe that understanding the ideas explored here will solve everything—what makes for a flourishing Church and lives transformed by the gospel is complex and multifaceted. But it does believe that greater clarity regarding the subject matter of this book will go a long way to help us regain our confidence in mission, and to rediscover how Christianity is electric, fresh, relevant, contemporary and radical!

The book comprises nine chapters, including this introduction. In the first chapter, we look at the ideas which underpin contemporary politics, regardless of political affiliation, through a brief introduction to political liberalism. We then turn our attention to the Church's liturgy, exploring how the liturgy is political and how we might refresh our experience of it (Chapter 2). Chapters 3 to 7 take a different aspect of the Church's liturgy in turn—morning prayer, baptism, eucharist, footwashing, and the funeral service—exploring the ways in which they lay down a challenge to contemporary politics, offering a vision of what it is to be human deeply at odds with contemporary norms. In the Conclusion, we return to the question of the Church's mission, asking what the implication of the book's argument is for future Church practice—including in relation to current debates about mission and how the Church is political. Each chapter includes questions for discussion

---

articles.php/2097/the-christian-priest-today-lecture-on-the-occasion-of-the-150th-anniversary-of-ripon-college-cuddesd.html>, accessed 23 September 2022.

and suggestions for further reading in case readers wish to study the book as part of a group.

We now offer a brief introduction to political liberalism—the ideas which dominate politics and society even though we are scarcely aware of this. We need to be clear what political liberalism says in order to see how Christianity says something very different.

For reflection or discussion

1. What is the most inspiring project (church or other) that you have been involved in? What made it inspiring?
2. What is the opening argument of the book and what are your initial thoughts about it?
3. What seems important to you as you think about the mission of God's Church today? What should its priorities be?

Further reading

Adrian Pabst, *The Demons of Liberal Democracy* (Cambridge and Medford, MA: Polity Press, 2019).

CHAPTER 1

Political liberalism

You will, no doubt, recall what they say about goldfish. They don't notice the water they swim in! That is, the water is all around them, so they don't notice it.

It feels a bit similar with political liberalism.

It is the political creed we swim in. It underpins all our politics—regardless of political party (i.e. whether Labour/Conservative, Democrat/Republican, all are underpinned by liberalism)—and yet we remain largely oblivious to the fact. We don't notice it.

For a number of reasons, this is a disadvantage. However, it is especially a disadvantage if we want to understand how Christianity says something radically different in comparison to mainstream norms.

So in this chapter we are going to engage in a very short lesson in political theory to clarify what political liberalism says. This will lay the foundation for our scrutiny, in subsequent chapters, of the Church's liturgy—and how it is political—as a means of injecting new life into the Church's mission.

One way to come at the subject matter of this chapter is to conceive of ourselves as being confronted with competing stories—put very simply, the liberal story and the Christian story. If we are not careful, the liberal story (which as we will discover is a false story) wins, and we end up either not hearing the Christian story or corrupting it as we start to speak of Christianity in ways which are not true to our inheritance of faith. Both outcomes are very common.

But we don't want this to be the case. We want to understand what political liberalism says—to identify its influence in our day-to-day lives, and in the assumptions of our media, our politicians and other actors, including ourselves—and then see how Christianity says something very different. This way, we will be clearer about Christianity's distinctiveness as we go forward in mission.

So what do we mean by political liberalism?

The story of political liberalism

At root, political liberalism is a philosophy concerned with how to organize society. It emerged in Europe in the seventeenth century and, historic and contemporary critiques aside, continues to be the dominant political creed in Western Europe and North America (though much less so elsewhere in the world).*

Liberal ideas, particularly associated with the English philosopher John Locke (1632–1704), emerged in response to the tendency of rulers to abuse their subjects (so-called royal absolutism) and in the aftermath of the so-called "wars of religion".

Inevitably, there is much complexity and disagreement as to what happened, but to cut a long story short, the founding fathers of political liberalism argued that society was too diverse to agree on "ends", to agree what the "good society" should look like. Instead, they said the best we can do is agree on "means", to agree an approach to decision-making that if followed will produce better rather than worse outcomes, and protect citizens from abuse by their rulers. Thus, political liberalism focuses on procedure (how you should organize things) rather than on ends (what the "good society" looks like)— because it says we are too diverse to agree on this.

Here it is easy to see how the founding fathers of political liberalism were influenced by the conflicts of their day (e.g. the "wars of religion"). That is, amid much bloodshed seemingly over whether the good society should be Catholic or Protestant, one can understand why those wrestling with how to bring peace might bypass the question of ends, choosing to focus on procedure instead.

---

*   I worked for many years in Vietnam, where the influences of political liberalism were superficial to non-existent!

That said, whether the "wars of religion" actually *were* wars of religion is contested. Or to put it another way, the mainstream interpretation of the so-called "wars of religion" is a political one, which has had profound implications for the standing of the Church. In the revisionist view, the emergence of liberal ideas is much more about the rise of nation states and their taking power from the Church, rather than liberalism simply being a clever (apolitical) solution to a practical challenge.*

The essence of political liberalism

Critical for political liberalism is the importance of maintaining *the freedom of the individual.* This is at the heart of its focus on procedure. Protect individual rights, it is argued, and even if people don't agree on ends, everything will be okay.

However, it is important to understand that political liberalism understands the individual in a particular way—what Bhikhu Parekh has referred to as "austere and minimalist terms". He writes:

> [Liberalism] abstracts the person from all [their] "contingent" and "external" relations with other

---

*   William T. Cavanaugh, *The Myth of Religious Violence: Secular Ideology and the Roots of Modern Conflict* (Oxford and New York: Oxford University Press, 2009).

people and nature, and defines the person as an essentially self-contained and solitary being ... unambiguously marked off from the "outside" world by [their] body.*

Moreover, individuals are understood as choosers, separated from their choices—that is, there is "me", and there are the choices "I" make.

This is all very well up to a point, and there is little doubt that political liberalism has taken us a long way, delivering many of the institutions which we hold dear. But there are significant problems. In this chapter, we highlight five of them.

First, it is not clear that human beings are individuals in the way that political liberalism says they are. The technical way of putting it is that political liberalism has a "false anthropology" of what it is to be human. Christianity, to anticipate future arguments, has a much richer understanding of what it means to be human, focused much more on the relationships in which we are embedded.

Second, it is not clear that we should give up on agreeing ends so quickly. Of course, society is diverse, but is there nothing we can say together about ends? Again, Christianity—in contrast to political liberalism—wants

---

* Bhikhu Parekh, "The Cultural Particularity of Liberal Democracy", in David Held (ed.), *Prospects for Democracy: North, South, East, West* (Cambridge and Malden, MA: Polity Press, 1993), p. 158.

to speak about ends. It believes that human beings do have goods in common. There is a common good.*

Third, it is unclear that political liberalism's emphasis on the freedom of the individual is ultimately a recipe for human flourishing. Critics of political liberalism have made a distinction between negative and positive liberty, arguing that political liberalism is only interested in negative liberty.

Negative liberty is a term coined by the political theorist Isaiah Berlin (1909–97) to refer to unrestrained personal choice and freedom from constraint, regulated only by an individual's conscience or where an action is prohibited by law.

Positive liberty, by contrast, is where people are helped towards a more strenuous kind of human flourishing which looks beyond the freedom to choose just because you can. Political liberalism has been criticized on the grounds that it upholds the notion of freedom of choice without schooling people in the grounds on which they might make good choices. To cite a rather trivial but pertinent example, we all know that back-to-back watching of TV on demand does not lead to fulfilment, especially if one watches on one's own—but we do it anyway. Christianity, in contrast to political liberalism,

---

* Nicholas Sagovsky and Peter McGrail (eds), *Together for the Common Good: Towards a National Conversation* (London: SCM Press, 2015).

has a lot to say about how we might be formed to make life-giving choices.*

Fourth, as the years have gone by, there is a sense in which the underlying principles of political liberalism (notably around individual freedom), though not bad in and of themselves, have been pushed so far that they have started to have a destructive effect. It is here that it has been argued that political liberalism is to blame for an erosion of trust and of the civic bonds which hold society together. The result is we are struggling to get on with each other, to deliberate, and overcome disagreement peaceably: witness the tone of political debate in the UK or the US in recent years. Political liberalism, so the argument goes, has been pushed too far.**

Fifth, against the backdrop of growing poverty and inequality in Europe and North America, questions have been raised about whether a politics founded on political liberalism is actually capable of delivering what it promises. Of course, cause and effect are difficult to ascertain, but there is something about the persistent and widening gap between rich and poor which raises questions about what a society founded on political liberalism is set up to deliver. Moreover, an emphasis

---

* John Milbank and Adrian Pabst, *The Politics of Virtue: Post-Liberalism and the Human Future* (London and New York: Rowman & Littlefield, 2016).

** Adrian Pabst, *The Demons of Liberal Democracy* (Cambridge and Medford, MA: Polity Press, 2019).

on individual freedom can seem rather hollow when your choices are limited by poverty or other forms of exclusion.* Freedom for whom, we might ask?

In this chapter, we have looked at the origins and essence of political liberalism, which crucially elevates the importance of maintaining the freedom of the individual. In turn, we have considered some serious problems with this worldview, namely its singular depiction of us as "atomized" individuals, its championing of "means" over "ends", its emphasis on individual freedom as a route to flourishing, its destructive impact on trust and cohesion, and its association with rising inequality.

Before we conclude this chapter, it is worth emphasizing what we are *not* saying.

In talking about political liberalism, we are being quite specific, talking about it in its theoretically correct sense. We are not talking about "liberal" in a generic, popular sense (i.e. someone with vaguely progressive ideas). Moreover, political liberalism should not be confused with theological liberalism—the liberal wing of the Church as contrasted with catholic or evangelical wings of the Church—although there is often some overlap between theological and political liberalism. Furthermore, we are not focused in this book on economic liberalism (the view that emphasizes the importance of allowing the market rather than the state

---

* Liberalism connects up with and feeds a particular kind of capitalism, so it is the combination of liberalism and capitalism which is producing the economic and social outcomes we are seeing.

to determine economic decision-making), although again, these different positions sometimes overlap.* Instead, we are talking specifically about political liberalism as the overarching ideology which shapes Western European and North American society.

To conclude, Christianity has distinctive views on nearly everything we have discussed in this chapter. It differs from political liberalism in its understanding of what it is to be human. It has much to say about ends— remember Christianity believes in goods in common. Moreover, Christianity believes that there is more to life than unfettered personal choice, regulated only by an individual's conscience or the law (negative freedom), and that we need to be formed in order to make good choices.

Christianity's distinctive world view is expressed in the Church's liturgies although we often don't notice this, thereby missing a critical opportunity to communicate how Christianity is electric, fresh, relevant, contemporary, radical, *and political*. It is to this task we now turn, beginning with an exploration of what we should expect when the Church gathers for worship, and why it is political.

* Malcolm Brown, *Tensions in Christian Ethics: An Introduction* (London: SPCK, 2011).

For reflection or discussion

1. How is the book defining political liberalism (and how is it not)? What are political liberalism's key ideas?
2. Do you think society is too diverse to agree on what the good society looks like? Does Christianity believe this?
3. Is freedom of choice always the greatest good?

Further reading

Patrick J. Deneen, *Why Liberalism Failed* (New Haven and London: Yale University Press, 2018).

Larry Siedentop, *Inventing the Individual: The Origins of Western Liberalism* (London: Penguin Books, 2015).

CHAPTER 2

Liturgy revisited

One of the joys of being a bishop's chaplain is you get to visit a different church nearly every week. While this brings with it an element of unfamiliarity—and occasionally unpredictability!—I nearly always returned home buoyed up, with a sense that God had been worshipped in a distinctive local expression of church. It is the breadth of Anglicanism—diverse local expressions embedded in particular places—that excites me.

And yet, as I sat next to the bishop, looking out at the congregation, I sometime wondered what was going on in people's heads. Why were they here? What had brought them to church this morning?

Of course, people's motives for going to church are varied, and that's quite all right. But for all of us there is a danger that we become so familiar with the words of the liturgy that we scarcely pay them any attention. They literally go over our heads before we enjoy a cup of coffee and a chat, and then return to our lives as if nothing has happened. Even if we allow for periods of dryness in the exercise of our faith, this surely can't be right!

But it raises the question of what's *supposed* to happen when the Church gathers for worship. What is worship about?

Of course, huge amounts have been written on this topic over many years, and this book does not attempt a comprehensive review.* Rather, it simply seeks to offer a brief and selective "refresher" of what we should expect when we gather for worship. We will also start to explore how the Church's liturgy is political, building on the discussion about political liberalism in the previous chapter. This will lay the foundations for subsequent chapters where we will delve more deeply into the political nature of specific acts of worship.

Some preliminaries

In this book, I am interested in a particular kind of worship, namely the Church of England's authorized liturgies as set out in *Common Worship* (itself the successor to earlier forms of service such as the *Book of Common Prayer* and the *Alternative Service Book*). In making this choice, I don't wish to sideline those not used to worshipping in this way. My choice is simply born of my own experience, which has been very rich.

---

*   For an overview, see Stephen Burns, *SCM Studyguide: Liturgy*, 2nd edn (London: SCM Press, 2018).

But I am hopeful that the ideas explored in this book will resonate with you, however you worship.

Nevertheless, there are certain characteristics of Anglican liturgical worship that are worth mentioning by way of a point of departure. These characteristics are not necessarily unique to Anglican worship, nor are they always present. But they are commonly found in Anglican worship.

So what are these characteristics?

First, Scripture is ever-present in Anglican worship insofar as we follow a lectionary of prescribed biblical readings, but also because our liturgies—the authorized words we use—draw heavily on Scripture. That is, the words we use are often lifted directly from the Bible.

Second, there is a certain discipline to Anglican liturgy, which is to say the words are chosen carefully to try and express what we believe—doctrinally—as a Church. The words are therefore the fruit of much prayer, reflection and scholarship over centuries. They are also expertly crafted and often very beautiful. Moreover, given that the words are chosen to try and express what the Church believes, our liturgies are not simply expressive of the feelings of worshippers on a given day.* This, given that feelings come and go, is surely a strength.

---

*   Paul Avis, "Prayer Book Use and Conformity", in Mark Chapman, Sathianathan Clarke and Martyn Percy (eds), *The Oxford Handbook of Anglican Studies* (Oxford: Oxford University Press, 2015), p. 136.

Against this backdrop, one can see from this why any kind of liturgical revision is fraught with controversy! Change the words and you may depart from what the Church has historically believed.

Sometimes people suggest that it must be very dull using the same words week in week out—although there is lots of choice and seasonal variation. But this isn't the case. The words, and the way in which the liturgy is structured, offer a framework within which worship is possible. Thus, the liturgy is an aid to worship. Furthermore, as the words of the liturgy and the particularity of our context or circumstances blend together, there are never-ending possibilities for fresh insight and new depths. And yet, of course, the danger is—as we have suggested—that familiarity with the words breeds indifference or inattentiveness.

Remaining alert and expectant in worship

If familiarity with our orders of service risks indifference or inattentiveness, how might we work to ensure this doesn't happen and refresh our experience of worship?

There are four key points, which will feed into the discussion of the political nature of worship.

The first is a point about gathering. When the Church gathers for worship, it does not do so on its own initiative. Rather, it gathers in response to God's continuing work of gathering his people to participate in the life of God.

Thus, the Church's gathering is always a response to God's prior action and is itself an act of worship.* Consequently, we should view our own churchgoing, however tentative or uncertain, in the same way.

The second point to note is that when we gather for worship we don't do so on our own, individually, but corporately—as members of the body of Christ. There is a huge amount to be said on this point—and we will explore it in more detail in later chapters. At this stage, all we need to note is that Christianity believes our truest identity as human beings is found in the body of Christ. Or, to put it differently, in Christianity, there is no "I" apart from the body.

Third, liturgy, or when we gather for worship, is not some kind of private, niche activity where we engage in unreal activity or make-believe. Rather, it is the most real thing that humans can do. It is worth pausing on this because that is not the way people tend to view it. *Worship is the most real thing humans do!* That is, liturgy offers a foretaste of God's continuing work of reconciliation and healing in the world and is paradigmatic of everything else we do.

Put another way, in worship we proclaim that God is the source of all life, the source of every good and perfect gift. This is an orientation deeply at odds with

---

*   Philip Kenneson, "Gathering: Worship, Imagination, and Formation", in Stanley Hauerwas and Samuel Wells (eds), *The Blackwell Companion to Christian Ethics*, 2nd edn (Malden, MA and Oxford: Blackwell Publishing, 2011), p. 60.

contemporary society, which implicitly or explicitly operates as if this is not the case. But to speak in this way—and to be formed by our liturgies week by week—reconfigures the way that we see the world. Taken seriously, therefore, liturgy relativizes all our other loyalties and commitments, and schools us in a new way of being in the world.*

Fourth, if all this is true, it ought to be clear that worship involves a transition—and potentially a life-changing one. Exploring this idea, some have made a distinction between ritual, understood as rule-governed, habitual, repetitive and formulaic behaviour, and liturgy. Ritual leaves you in the same place. Liturgy is not liturgy unless it involves a transition:

> [L]iturgy is an *event* in a physical space that has
> the effect of moving you from one context or
> condition of heart and imagination to another.**

Rowan Williams develops this point, focusing on the fact that we are embodied beings and experience our lives as shaped through time. This observation notwithstanding, he notes we live in a culture which is often deeply illiterate about the body and which has

---

*   Ibid., p. 62.
**   Rowan Williams, Introduction, "*Common Worship*, common life: defining liturgy for today", in Nicholas Papadopulos (ed.), *God's Transforming Work: Celebrating Ten Years of* Common Worship (London: SPCK, 2011), p. 2.

a one-dimensional view of time as simply something that needs to be filled up. Liturgy, by contrast, is about the transformation of the "time-taking body within the material world".* Williams goes on:

> It may seem strange to speak of illiteracy about the body in a culture which appears very interested indeed in material gratification of all kinds ... and yet the notion that bodies are *organs of meaning* is not one that is easy to explain in our present context ... Likewise we find difficulty in seeing and feeling the passage of time as meaningful; we are, very largely, trapped in *undifferentiated* time; we don't know how to *mark* time.**

Liturgy seeks to extend our understanding of time, and what it is to be embodied, both of which are integral to a full understanding of our humanity. At its best, liturgy seeks to show us how the body is a "signifying" or "meaning" reality. It seeks to show us that liturgical time is the opposite of time that just has to be filled up. Williams again:

> [Liturgical time] is the time of a drama, the time of an event. It is thus to do with the building and releasing of tension, and the time needed

---

*   Ibid., p. 11.
**   Ibid., p. 3.

for transition to happen. It is differentiated time,
time that has a "shape" to it and as such it casts
a different light on how we spend the rest of our
time (or at least it should).*

For this reason, we should resist the tendency always to try and make liturgy more accessible within contemporary society (although some consideration of this is clearly to be encouraged). Rather, we should remember that good liturgy is addressed to people who do not yet exist.**

So far in this chapter, we have noted a number of things intended to refresh our experience of worship and keep us alert and expectant. First, that worship is a response to God's prior action. Second, that we gather corporately, not on our own. Third, that worship is the most real thing we do: it relativizes all our other loyalties and commitments, and changes the way we see the world. Fourth, that worship should involve a transition from one context or perspective to another, deepening our understanding of what it is to be embodied and for our lives to be shaped through time. In turn, worship should change the way we "spend" the rest of "our" time.

There is, of course, much more to be said about all these things, and subsequent chapters will enable us to do so. However, we now turn to the other important question of this chapter, namely, how then is liturgy political?

---

*   Ibid., p. 8.
** Ibid., p. 10.

The political nature of worship

Put simply, liturgy is political because it tells a story about the nature of the world and our place in it which is profoundly at odds with political liberalism, the dominant creed by which we live in Europe and North America. This is the particular point that this book is making. We got a hint of it earlier in the chapter when we saw how Christianity, through its liturgy, reconfigures the way we see the world and our place in it. Stories or ideas are always political. The Church's ideas—its doctrines—expressed in its liturgies tell a story that rejects the tenets of political liberalism and therefore they are political.

But note, we are *not* talking about narrow party politics which, regardless of political party, is always in thrall to political liberalism. Rather, to speak of politics in this way—separate and distinct from party politics— is to strive for a contribution by the Church to public life which clarifies the Church's distinctive message. This goes beyond both the "stay-out-of-politics" camp and the tendency to jump on every contemporary bandwagon without adequate engagement with our inheritance of faith. Both positions are mistaken and fall short of what Christianity has to offer the world. In this book, we are striving for a distinctive contribution to public life which is to be found in a careful reading of the Church's liturgy. We will return to this in the Conclusion.

Notwithstanding a diversity of positions, there is, on the whole, much resistance to viewing the Church—let alone its liturgies—as political. People will comment, for example, if a vicar or a bishop is seen to be "too political". That this is the case has a long and complex history which goes beyond the scope of this book. But put briefly, it is a story of the Church conceding ground—and losing confidence—over many centuries, beginning with the conversion of Constantine to Christianity in the fourth century and continuing through the onset of modernity and the rise of the secular liberal state itself.

One of the things Christians need to do in the face of this history is to notice our reluctance to view the Church, and especially its liturgies, as political, and to reclaim the space but in a way which draws on the deep well of the Church's theology rather than on political liberal norms. Note that this is not something we should be shrill or arrogant about, but rather we need to reflect carefully, noting nevertheless that there are important things at stake. In subsequent chapters, we will start to put some flesh on the bones of this argument, looking at a number of different liturgies in turn.

Before we conclude this chapter, it is important to make one final point about the nature of liturgy. The focus of this book is on the *ideas* contained in the Church's liturgy. However, while those ideas are of crucial importance, they are not the whole story. Liturgy is an event. It is something we *do*. It is something which involves all the senses. Put another way, there is no such thing as a generic baptism or a generic service of Holy Communion, only actual services where people gather in a particular time and place.* This book's focus is on the ideas contained in the liturgy notwithstanding, but we do not forget this. However, the hope is that a focus on the one will be in service of the other.

Let us turn to our first chapter where we focus on one particular part of the Church's liturgy.

For reflection or discussion

1. What makes an act of worship (or liturgy) a good act of worship?
2. What is implied by the suggestion that good liturgy should be addressed to people who do not exist?
3. In what way is the Church's liturgy political? Political in what sense? How do you feel about this?

Further reading

Stephen Burns, *SCM Studyguide: Liturgy*, 2nd edn (London: SCM Press, 2018).

---

* Bryan Spinks, "Worship", in John Webster, Kathryn Tanner and Iain Torrance (eds), *The Oxford Handbook of Systematic Theology* (Oxford and New York: Oxford University Press, 2007), pp. 378–93.

CHAPTER 3

Morning Prayer

I first started attending Morning Prayer when I was exploring a possible call to ordained ministry. When getting out of bed in the morning didn't feel too inviting, I could drag myself down to the Cathedral for Morning Prayer with the promise of a cup of coffee afterwards. In the early days, I used to take the dog—a somewhat unpredictable Border Collie called Jonah—who I would tie up in the Cathedral porch. More than once, Morning Prayer was interrupted by the sound of Jonah barking at the passers-by!

As the years have gone by, I have persisted with Morning Prayer, enjoying the discipline and fellowship of it with colleagues. But I know, too, the temptation to skip it when the business of the day is bearing down on you. Yet I have learnt that it is precisely when I feel inclined to skip Morning Prayer that I need it most.

In this chapter, we explore what happens when one enters into the practice of Morning Prayer. The argument is that Morning Prayer refocuses our attention such that we start to see the world, and our place in it, more truthfully, in turn strengthening our ability to make judgements which are more in tune with God's purposes. That, at least, is the theory!

Whatever liturgical season we are in, the opening words of Morning Prayer are always the same:

O Lord, open our lips

To which the response is:

and our mouth shall proclaim your praise.

Focusing on these very first words—"O Lord, open our lips"—notice that it is God, we acknowledge, who opens our lips. That is, this simple action involving just five words created by lips, tongue and breath is not possible without God. Without God's creative energy, I cannot say the words. I am dependent on God even for my breath.

Notice too how our speaking at the start of Morning Prayer recalls God's first action recorded in the book Genesis as God *spoke* the created order into existence. The refrain "And God said" is repeated again and again in Genesis 1.

Notice also how we don't say "O Lord, open *my* lips". Rather, we say "O Lord, open *our* lips", creating a sense from the very beginning of the liturgy that we gather for prayer in relationship with others (those physically present, those who have gone before us, those gathering elsewhere for prayer).

And what is our response to this call upon God to open our lips at the beginning of a new day? It is, as we saw, to commit to praise God, the one who spoke the created order into being:

> and our mouth shall proclaim your praise.

Before we have got more than two seconds into Morning Prayer, we have done two things: we have acknowledged our dependency on God even for the simple act of breath and moving our lips and tongue, and we have asserted that the correct response to this is to praise God.

What happens next?

Following these opening words, we move into a prayer of thanksgiving—and again, regardless of where we are in the liturgical calendar, Morning Prayer always continues with thanksgiving. For example:

> Bless the Lord, O my soul,
> and all that is within me bless his holy name.
>> *Psalm 103:1*

Or:

> O Lord our governor,
> how glorious is your name in all the world!
>> *Psalm 8:1*

Having recited a prayer of thanksgiving to God, we then say an opening prayer. The first part of the prayer acknowledges the passing of the night, where in the tradition of Night Prayer (Compline) we have asked for God's protection:

> Save us, O Lord, while waking,
> and guard us while sleeping,
> that awake we may watch with Christ
> and asleep may rest in peace.

Having noted in our opening prayer that "The night has passed, and the day lies open before us", we then hold a short period of silence before acknowledging—and rejoicing—that each new day is *a gift* from God in which we participate, and to which we commit in prayer:

> As we rejoice in the gift of this new day,
> so may the light of your presence, O God,
> set our hearts on fire with love for you;
> now and for ever. Amen.

Next comes the heart of Morning Prayer, when we listen to and recite God's word in a series of Psalms, Bible passages and canticles drawn from Scripture, before offering prayers of intercession to God for the day and its tasks, the world and its needs, and for the Church and her life. Note that it is God's word we listen to or recite, not our own!

So, to recap, in Morning Prayer we gather with others (those present and those not). We acknowledge our dependence on God. We commit ourselves to praise God. We give thanks. We hold silence. We listen to and recite God's word (not our own), and we pray. Only then do we move to attend to the business of the day!

So what is the meaning of this?

The American Jewish writer Peter Ochs, looking at Morning Prayer in the Jewish tradition, argues that Morning Prayer trains us in "redemptive thinking", by which he means teaching us to make judgements which are more in tune with God.[*] He notes, by contrast, the predominance of "propositional logic" in the modern West (I do A to B, or I believe X is y) where, in effect, we rush to judgement based on *my* perspective or *my* worldview. Ochs doesn't dismiss propositional logic out of hand—indeed, seen through the lens of science it has served us well—but he is rightly concerned if this is the only logic at work.

We can see how Christian Morning Prayer, as with its Jewish counterpart, trains us in "redemptive thinking", stopping us in our tracks, or at least slowing us down, as we start to see our position in the world, and the judgements we make, differently.

But let's unpack this a little more.

---

[*] Peter Ochs, "Morning Prayer as Redemptive Thinking", in Randi Rashkover and C.C. Pecknold (eds), *Liturgy, Time, and the Politics of Redemption* (Grand Rapids, MI: Eerdmans, and London: SCM Press, 2006), pp. 50–87.

The first point to make is that through the act of saying Morning Prayer, we remember the God who is faithful to us even when we don't remember him. We see that the world is a "collective of creatures who are spoken to and speak" and that I am just one of them in a long history of souls present and past.* And we see our lives in the context of a much bigger story of God's action in the world, told and retold through Scripture. And, through all this, our sense of who we are, and the contingency of our thoughts and our actions, is relativized: "I am what is not mine . . . the essence of what I am is not mine."**

Or, as one of the responsories in Morning Prayer expresses it:

> Trust in the Lord with all your heart;
> and be not wise in your own sight.

Put another way, Morning Prayer opens up a space where we are deterred from rushing to judgement. Indeed, it reminds us that we are ourselves judged (Psalm 103:6). Instead, Morning Prayer opens up a space for "discernment" in the true sense of that word, where we listen and where we wait on God in order *to be shown*—rather than rushing headlong into the day's tasks, making hasty judgements of "our own".

And yet, while this may inject a certain helpful humility and contingency in the way we relate to the

---

*   Ibid., p. 78.

**   Abraham J. Heschel, cited in ibid., p. 59.

world, we do not surrender through Morning Prayer our ability to act altogether. Rather, our capacity to act is "preserved in its nobility" as we realize that the creator of the universe is concerned with us:*

> When I consider your heavens, the
>   work of your fingers,
> the moon and the stars that you have ordained,
> What are mortals, that you should
>   be mindful of them;
> mere human beings, that you should seek them out?
>
> *Psalm 8:3–4*

And what a joy, a relief and a source of energy that it doesn't all depend on us, given the complexities and challenges life throws at us!

While we've not laboured the point in this chapter, we can see clearly how the political liberal idea of the individual as a "contained self", which we identified in the first chapter, is not remotely recognized in the liturgy of Morning Prayer. We will expand on this idea (that Christianity sees the world very differently from political liberalism) as the book unfolds, not least in the next chapter, on baptism.

---

*   Ibid., p. 85.

For reflection or discussion

1. How do you start the day?
2. Why, according to the chapter, might prayer in the morning be helpful for a disciple of Jesus?
3. What is the significance of the opening words of Morning Prayer ("O Lord, open our lips") and the response?
4. How does the service of Morning Prayer challenge the liberal idea of an individual as a contained self?

Further reading

John Pritchard, *How to Pray: A Practical Handbook* (London: SPCK, 2002).

Rowan Williams, "Prayer", in Rowan Williams, *Being Christian: Baptism, Bible, Eucharist, Prayer* (London: SPCK, 2014), pp. 61–82.

CHAPTER 4

Baptism

In the opening words of the baptism service in the *Book of Common Prayer*, there is a startling phrase in which the priest asks the congregation to call upon God to grant to the person being baptized "that thing which by nature he [*sic*] cannot have".* The phrase harks back to an understanding of baptism which is easily lost in our contemporary setting, namely that baptism is not ultimately something that we do or choose, rather it is something God does. Moreover, the reference to "that thing which by nature [we] cannot have" reminds us of the classical but still pertinent understanding of baptism that it releases us from our "inherited sins". That is, sins inherited from Adam at the time of the Fall, by virtue of the fact that like Adam, we are human beings (Romans 5:12–21). No decision or act of ours can release us from our sins.

---

* *The Book of Common Prayer, and Administration of the Sacraments, and other Rites and Ceremonies of the Church, according to the use of the Church of England* (Cambridge: Cambridge University Press, Standard Edition), p. 264.

The *Book of Common Prayer* speaks forcefully of baptism as "utterly abolish[ing] the whole body of sin". In the opening prayer for the baptism service, *Common Worship* says the same thing, albeit with gentler language:

> Our Lord Jesus Christ has told us
> that to enter the kingdom of heaven
> we must be born again of water and the Spirit,
> and has given us baptism as the sign
>   and seal of this new birth.
> Here we are washed by the Holy
>   Spirit and made clean.
> Here we are clothed with Christ,
> dying to sin that we may live his risen life.

While this emphasis on what happens in baptism is a helpful reminder in today's individualistic climate, there is something else which is in danger of being lost and that is how Christianity understands the body— what it is to be a self—fundamentally differently from liberal norms with which we are more familiar. For the Christian, in language which is undoubtedly challenging for liberal ears, our body is not something we control as a "self-enclosed private domain" but rather "something shared because it is something surrendered to the Spirit of God".* It is these ideas which I will unpack in this chapter.

---

* Frederick Christian Bauerschmidt, "Being Baptized: Bodies and Abortion", in Stanley Hauerwas and Samuel Wells (eds), *The Blackwell*

While there are a number of different elements to the baptism service, the chapter focuses on just two of them—when the baptism candidate is signed with the cross and the moment of baptism itself—exploring how this "sharing" and "surrendering", referred to above, occurs and how it can be understood. In the previous chapter, we said that the liberal idea of the individual as a "contained self" is not recognized in Christianity. This chapter goes a step further to unpack more precisely how the self is understood through the baptism service.

Signing of the cross

In *Common Worship*, the priest's signing of the cross on the baptism candidate's forehead occurs after they have been presented to the congregation, and after either they, or their parents or godparents, have declared their commitment to turn to Christ and repent of their sins in the words of the so-called Decision. Making the sign of the cross, the priest says:

> Christ claims you for his own.
> Receive the sign of his cross.

Companion to Christian Ethics, 2nd edn (Malden, MA, Oxford and Carlton, Victoria: Blackwell Publishing, 2011), p. 254.

Moreover, the signing of the cross on the forehead is the first of two occasions when the baptism candidate is touched.

So what is going on here?

That the baptism candidate's body is touched is not without significance in terms of how the body is recast through the liturgy. "Repeatedly", says Frederick Bauerschmidt, the body of the candidate is touched during baptism so that "through touch it may be incorporated into the ecclesial Body of Christ".* Incorporation into the body of Christ is a key way in which the baptized body is understood differently from the liberal body—not as an isolated individual but part of a collective, intimately related to one's neighbour, to the Church, and to God. As St Paul says in his extended treatise on "the body with many parts":

> For just as the body is one and has many members, and all the members of the body, though many, are one body, so it is with Christ. For in the one Spirit we were all baptized into one body . . . If all were a single member, where would the body be?
>
> *1 Corinthians 12:12–13,19*

And then, further emphasizing our interdependence as human beings:

---

*   Ibid., p. 253.

> If one member suffers, all suffer together with it;
> if one member is honoured, all rejoice together
> in it.
>
> *1 Corinthians 12:26*

Given the history of the Church, this emphasis on the importance of touch in baptism may raise concerns about the potential for abuse. However, properly understood, this is not a grasping touch or one that seeks to dominate or control. Rather, it is a touch of welcome. Indeed, in *Common Worship*, the signing of the cross is preceded by an invitation to the congregation to welcome the candidate:

> People of God, will you welcome
> these *children/candidates*
> and uphold *them* in *their* new life in Christ?

Moreover, the best guard against abuse is that the touch is communal—in *Common Worship* not just the priest but the parents and godparents can be invited to make the sign of the cross on the candidate's forehead. The touch is also cruciform, symbolizing, as the cross of Christ does, a renunciation of control more in tune with God's freedom:

> The cross and the community make it clear that
> the baptized body is a body subjected not to any

human individual, whether priest or parent, but
to God and God alone.*

This section of the baptism service finishes with words
of exorcism:

> May almighty God deliver you from
>   the powers of darkness,
> restore in you the image of his glory,
> and lead you in the light and obedience of Christ.

While some may see this as a superstitious hangover
from earlier times, another way to view it is as a prayer
aimed at freeing the body of the illusion that we are in
control—leading us away from the powers of darkness
into the light. Bauerschmidt says that this illusion of
control is "perhaps the chief spirit that must be cast out"
in baptism, arguing that through baptism we are aiming
for a different kind of self-possession:**

> For all things are yours . . . all belong to you,
> and you belong to Christ, and Christ belongs
> to God.
>
>   *1 Corinthians 3:21–23*

Again, we should emphasize the communal nature of
the touch and the way in which baptism is about moving

---

*   Ibid., p. 255.

**   Ibid., p. 256.

away from a sense of our bodies being a "self-enclosed private domain" towards one open to the Holy Spirit: once again, the touch must come from the community of those "who view neither their individual bodies nor their collective body as a space that they control, but as a space for the radical hospitality of the Spirit".*

Baptism with water

The next occasion when the baptismal candidate is touched—this time by water—is when the congregation gathers around the font, or the full immersion pool, for the baptism itself. This act is preceded by the prayer over the water in which we remember the role of water in God's saving actions:

> We thank you, almighty God, for the gift of water
> to sustain, refresh and cleanse all life.
> Over water the Holy Spirit moved in
>   the beginning of creation.
> Through water you led the children of Israel
> from slavery in Egypt to freedom
>   in the Promised Land.
> In water your Son Jesus received the baptism of John
> and was anointed by the Holy Spirit
>   as the Messiah, the Christ,
> to lead us from the death of sin to newness of life.

---

*   *Idem.*

Unpacking this, we can see the way in which a series of boundaries are unsettled. In this moment, as the prayer is read, there is no division between the water in this font, or this baptismal pool, and the waters over which the Spirit moved at creation, the waters of the Red Sea, or of the Jordan in which Jesus was baptized. Bauerschmidt even makes a connection between the water and blood that flowed from Jesus' side at his crucifixion, underlining a further unsettling of boundaries, this time between Jesus and the candidate for baptism. He writes:

> By entering into the water that flows from Christ's body, the candidate will become one with that body, as if the baptismal water will erode the boundaries between the candidate's body and the body of Christ.*

Thus, through the touch of water, the baptismal candidate becomes one with Jesus' body.

Noting water as both a chaotic and dangerous element and a source of life, it is in the font (or baptism pool) that the baptismal body is finally transformed—as the old self is dissolved and the new self is born. In order to be born again, we must first die with Christ:

> We thank you, Father, for the water of baptism.
> In it we are buried with Christ in his death.
> By it we share in his resurrection.

---

* Ibid., p. 257.

As with Christ's death and the three days of waiting, there is a moment of suspense as the candidate is dipped or plunged into the water, which is only brought to a conclusion by the priest speaking in the name of the triune God:

> I baptize you
> in the name of the Father,
> and of the Son,
> and of the Holy Spirit.
> Amen.

Underlining the transformation that has taken place in the baptized body, *Common Worship* allows at this point for the optional putting on of a white robe with the words:

> You have been clothed with Christ.
> As many as are baptized into Christ
>   have put on Christ.

This language of "being clothed with Christ" or having "put Christ on" further captures that sense of a changed relationship between the baptized body and Jesus and the wider community of the Church, moving us yet further from the liberal idea of the private individual.

With this part of the service concluded, the newly baptized candidate is commissioned to live out the story with which they have been marked, by extending the welcome they have received from God and the Church to others. Then prayers of intercession are said and the one newly baptized is sent out with a lighted candle and with words that recall the prayer of exorcism earlier in the service:

> God has delivered us from the dominion of darkness
> and has given us a place with the saints in light.
> . . . Shine as a light in the world
> to the glory of God the Father.

I remember one particular baptism where the child was strong and restless—more a toddler than an infant. The years since I had handled my own small children having passed some time before, I chose the safer option of asking the mother to hold her child while I poured the water over their head. Looking back, while I am sure it didn't invalidate the baptism, I feel I conceded ground unhelpfully in terms of the argument of this chapter. It is through the communal and cruciform touch of the Church—at the signing of the cross and with water—that the baptized body is recast. We are no longer a private "liberal" self, but rather a body filled with God's Spirit—connected to Jesus, our neighbour and the Church.

In the next chapter, we look at how the service of Holy Communion (or Eucharist) further challenges the sensibilities of political liberalism.

For reflection or discussion

1. What do you remember, or what do you know, about your baptism?
2. What do you make of the idea that baptism is not something we do or choose, rather that it is something God does? Do we get this emphasis right in our baptism services and what is the danger if we don't?
3. Why, according to this chapter, is touch important in the baptism service?
4. How is the baptized body understood differently from the liberal body?

Further reading

Angela Tilby, "Whatever happened to original sin?", in Nicholas Papadopoulos (ed.), *God's Transforming Work: Celebrating Ten Years of* Common Worship (London: SPCK, 2011), pp.35–50.

Rowan Williams, "Baptism", in Rowan Williams, *Being Christian: Baptism, Bible, Eucharist, Prayer* (London: SPCK, 2014), pp. 1–19.

CHAPTER 5

Eucharist

Picture the scene. It's election time. Two political parties—the frontrunners—are slogging it out trying to win over the electorate. Vote for us and we'll deliver lower taxes, says one. Vote for us and we'll deliver stronger public services, says the other. The leaders of the main political parties agree to a televised debate. It is customarily fractious with both accusing the other of peddling a false narrative. Insults are exchanged, but commentators judge the outcome of the TV debate as inconclusive. Only election day will tell!

With reference to the above scenario, we don't have any difficulty seeing this as politics (though it is a fairly narrow conception of politics). For one political party to describe their rival's narrative as false is patently political. Stories about the way things *are* matter in politics—they need to be believed. Being told that the narrative of your political party is false is a political act, bound to precipitate a response as the impugned party seeks to reassert its credibility.

In this chapter, we are making a similar claim that the narrative Christianity tells is political, because through the Eucharist it tells a radically different story from the dominant liberal one. Although—unlike the scenario above—for reasons we touched on in Chapter 2, we tend not to see it like this.

The chapter is in two parts. We first contrast the liberal story with the Christian story, drawing on work by the American author William Cavanaugh.* This first section sets out how the two stories see the world, and what it is to be human in it, in fundamentally different ways. We then look at how the Christian story is expressed liturgically in the Eucharist as set out in *Common Worship*. The argument is that when we receive communion, we are not just remembering what Christ did in some vague ethereal way. Rather, we become united with Christ, and our sense of who is our neighbour is transformed. This, in turn, sets us up for a radically different way of being in the world from that perpetuated by the liberal story.

---

* William T. Cavanaugh, "The City: Beyond secular parodies", in John Milbank, Catherine Pickstock and Graham Ward (eds), *Radical Orthodoxy: A New Theology* (London and New York: Routledge, 1999), pp. 182–200.

The liberal story

William Cavanaugh writes about the political nature of the Eucharist when he contrasts the Christian story with what he calls the "state story" (for our purposes, the liberal story). Echoing arguments we made in Chapter 1, Cavanaugh says that the liberal story is founded on the "essential individuality of the human race". He quotes the political philosopher Jean-Jacques Rousseau (1712–78) who famously said that "human beings are born free", and adds that what Rousseau meant is "free primarily from each other".*

So the liberal story, in terms of its fundamental beliefs about human nature, sees human beings at root as being disconnected or separate from each other. Moreover, according to this view, humans are liable to fight or interfere with each other's rights, unless they are suitably ordered and disciplined by government.

It is classically this understanding of the world which led to the emergence of the liberal state. Thomas Hobbes (1588–1679), another political philosopher associated with the emergence of liberalism, imagined a kind of "state of nature", where he says people will "want what only one [individual] can have". It is on this basis that Rousseau's so-called "social contract" emerged, where citizens concede power to the state in return for protection of self (and property). As we saw in Chapter

---

*   Ibid., p. 186.

1, these ideas continue to underpin our politics to this
day—regardless of political party.

The Christian story

The Christian story, by contrast, starts in an entirely
different place from the liberal one. Instead of speaking
of the individuality of the human race, it recalls the
"natural unity" of human beings going back to the
creation of humankind, described in Genesis, where
humans are made in the image of God.

To speak in this way is not to engage in a literal
reading of the Genesis story, but it is to read Genesis
as saying something fundamental about what it is to be
human. According to the Christian story, it was Adam's
disobedience that shattered the natural unity of the
human race, further illustrated in the stories of Cain and
Abel, the Great Flood, and the Tower of Babel, which
are symbolic of humanity's divisions and its setting itself
up in the place of God.

But in response, the Christian story doesn't say
human beings need protecting from each other, as does
the liberal story. Rather, our true nature—our freedom
and our redemption—is found in recovering our natural
unity, by participating in God and one another.

Indeed, one reading of the Christian story is that
before the Fall the idea of the individual makes no
sense. Cavanaugh writes that "the effect of sin is the very

creation of individuals as such".* Prior to the Fall, united in God and one another, there could be no distinction between what is mine and what is yours.

It is here that Paul's writing about the body of Christ in 1 Corinthians 12 is evocative. We are not members *individually* of the body, says Paul, but rather "cohere to each other as in a natural body". Similarly, while the body has weaker and stronger members, we are not separate from each other but "participate in each other" such that my wellbeing is intimately bound up with your wellbeing and vice versa.

Speaking about the contrast between the Christian story and the liberal story, Cavanaugh describes the liberal story as a false copy of the Christian story. Indeed, it mimics the Christian story by promising to save us— whether by preventing our differences getting out of hand, lowering taxes or providing better public services. But the liberal story can never truly deliver—it offers a false unity and a false peace—because it misunderstands what it means to be human.

As we have seen, the liberal story believes in the individuality of the human race and the need to be protected from each other. Therefore, it keeps us apart and cannot unite us. Only through participation in the body of Christ, says Christianity, can we overcome the things which divide us and discover the goods we have in common.

---

* Ibid., p. 184.

Having contrasted the liberal and the Christian story, we now turn to how these ideas are expressed in the liturgy of the Eucharist. The hope is that we will now see more clearly how, through the story it tells, the Eucharist is political.

The liturgy of the Eucharist

The Order for the Celebration of Holy Communion in *Common Worship* (also called The Eucharist and The Lord's Supper) is divided into four principal parts: the Gathering, the Liturgy of the Word, the Liturgy of the Sacrament and the Dismissal. While important things happen in all four parts of the service, it is the Liturgy of the Sacrament, and particularly the Eucharistic Prayer(s), which we will focus on here.

The Liturgy of the Sacrament begins with the Peace, after which the table is prepared and the gifts of bread and wine are presented. The Peace is a key moment— we greet each other, acknowledging our common humanity. Matthew's Gospel reminds us forcefully of the importance of being reconciled with our neighbour before receiving communion, even if this is a standard with which we may struggle:

> So when you are offering your gift at the altar,
> if you remember that your brother or sister has
> something against you, leave your gift there

before the altar and go; first be reconciled to
your brother or sister, and then come and offer
your gift.

Matthew 5:23–24

But the Peace is also a turning point in the service at
which momentum builds as we prepare to remember
what Jesus has done for us, before moving into the
Eucharistic Prayer:

The Lord is here.
His Spirit is with us.
Lift up your hearts.
We lift them to the Lord.

and so on . . .

Common Worship gives us eight different options
for the Eucharistic Prayer, in the interests of variety
(Prayers A–H). They nearly all begin by acknowledging
the importance of giving thanks and praise, picking
up on themes present in the opening responses of the
Eucharistic Prayer:

It is indeed right,
it is our duty and our joy,
at all times and in all places
to give you thanks and praise.

"Eucharist", from the Greek *eucharisto*, means "I give thanks."

The Eucharistic Prayer(s) then offer an impressively concise "Christian story in miniature", covering the bases of creation, fall, incarnation (Jesus coming amongst us), his death, resurrection, and our redemption. Prayer F is a particularly good example:

> You fashioned us in your image
> and placed us in the garden of your delight.
> Though we chose the path of rebellion
> you would not abandon your own.
> . . .
> Embracing our humanity,
> Jesus showed us the way of salvation;
> loving us to the end,
> he gave himself to death for us;
> dying for his own,
> he set us free from the bonds of sin,
> that we might rise and reign with him in glory.

Then, as the Eucharistic Prayer builds to a crescendo, certain themes relevant to the argument of this chapter are emphasized again and again.

First and foremost, we are told that as we share the bread and wine (ingest Christ's body and blood), we are made one in Christ—with echoes of a return to the situation before the Fall. The diversity of images deployed in the various Eucharistic Prayers help to express this. We are "united", "gathered", "formed" and "made one", but the message is clear:

> . . . as we eat and drink these holy gifts
> in the presence of your divine majesty,
> renew us by your Spirit,
> inspire us with your love
> and unite us in the body of your Son,
> Jesus Christ our Lord.
>
> *Prayer A*

Or:

> As we eat and drink these holy gifts
> make us one in Christ, our risen Lord.
>
> *Prayer H*

However, as one hears the story told and retold, it is not just that we are united with Christ through partaking in his body and blood. More than this, we catch a glimpse of a changed relationship with our neighbour too—reconciled, not divided as in the liberal body. This is expressed most clearly at the breaking of the bread:

> Though we are many, we are one body,
> because we all share in one bread.

And yet there is more still.

It is not only that through the Eucharist we are united to our neighbour and made one with Christ in the here and now. In addition, we catch a glimpse of a vision of reconciliation that extends across time and space, connecting us to those who have gone before us and looking ahead to the heavenly banquet at the end of the age:

> Gather your people from the ends of the earth
> to feast with all your saints
> at the table in your kingdom,
> where the new creation is brought to perfection ...
>
> *Prayer F*

Or:

> Bring us at the last with all the saints
> to the vision of that eternal splendour
> for which you have created us;
>
> *Prayer G*

Surely this is the ultimate riposte to the divided liberal body: an expression of commonality and unity which knows no bounds. No narrow nationalism or bipartisanship here, but a uniting of all peoples in Christ's body across time and space:

> Then people will come from east and west, from
> north and south, and will eat in the kingdom
> of God.
>
> *Luke 13:29*

> There is no longer Jew or Greek, there is no
> longer slave or free, there is no longer male and
> female; for all of you are one in Christ Jesus.
>
> *Galatians 3:28*

And finally, we are sent out into the world with the
Prayer after Communion ringing in our ears:

> May we who share Christ's body live his risen life;
> we who drink his cup bring life to others;
> we whom the Spirit lights give light to the world.

So what does this add up to?

In this chapter, we have highlighted the way in
which, contrary to the way we usually view it, the
Eucharist is deeply political. This is because it tells a
story of the essential unity of the human race—what
we have in common—and thereby is at loggerheads
with the dominant liberal story, with its emphasis on
the separateness of human beings and their need to be
protected from each other. While we often live out the
liberal story, clamouring for our rights, deep down we
recognize the connection we have with each other, and
that the liberal story peddles a false anthropology of

what it is to be human. We explore these issues further in the next chapter, on footwashing.

For reflection or discussion

1. " . . . if you remember that your brother or sister has something against you . . . first be reconciled to your brother or sister, and then come and offer your gift." (Matthew 5:23–4). What does this tell us about the nature of Holy Communion?
2. How do the Christian and the liberal stories differ in terms of their fundamental understanding of what it is to be human?
3. In what ways are Christianity's foundational ideas about humanity expressed in the Communion liturgy?
4. How might what we learn from partaking in Communion help us as we think about contemporary politics?

Further reading

John Hadley, *Bread of the World: Christ and the Eucharist Today* (London: Darton, Longman & Todd, 1989).

Rowan Williams, "Eucharist", in Rowan Williams, *Being Christian: Baptism, Bible, Eucharist, Prayer* (London: SPCK, 2014), pp. 41–60.

CHAPTER 6

Footwashing

*And during supper Jesus, knowing that the Father
had given all things into his hands, and that he
had come from God and was going to God, got
up from the table, took off his outer robe, and tied
a towel around himself. Then he poured water
into a basin and began to wash the disciples' feet
and to wipe them with the towel that was tied
around him.*

John 13:2b–5

It is from this account of Jesus washing his disciples'
feet, unique to John's Gospel, that the Church receives
the liturgy of footwashing, which commonly takes place
on Maundy Thursday. Having washed his disciples' feet,
Jesus instructs them to wash each other's feet and issues
a new commandment (Latin *mandatum*—from which
the word Maundy comes), to love one another: "By this
everyone will know that you are my disciples," Jesus says
(John 13:12–15,34–35).

Mention footwashing to your average churchgoer, however, and it is quite likely you will elicit a groan or a "rather-you-than-me" response. Our feet are dirty, private, gnarled from the slog of life, and we'd rather not have our vicar see them, let alone touch them. Moreover, when the Church does engage in footwashing, it is often a sanitized affair as likely to reinforce existing social hierarchies as challenge them.

Furthermore, footwashing in our churches today is not really washing at all, with people warned in advance (hence able to scrub their feet and put on their best socks!) and water simply poured, often on just one foot which is then patted dry with a towel.

Or, departing still further from the practice Jesus mandated us to do, we instead wash hands or shine shoes to spare people's blushes. All this is unfortunate—a good example of how we like our liturgy tethered and domesticated—with the meaning and radical nature of what is at stake undoubtedly lost.

Jesus, on the other hand, is clear that footwashing is of defining importance in the life of a disciple, saying without compromise in the face of Simon Peter's resistance to having his feet washed, "Unless I wash you, you have no share with me" (John 13:8). No share with Jesus? That's strong: you can't get clearer than that!

In this chapter, we explore what is being communicated through the act of footwashing—given to us by Jesus—and why it is important. We offer an initial note on the place of footwashing in Jesus' day, before unpacking where it sits in the liturgy today. Then we immerse ourselves in the text of John 13, as the best place to get a handle on what footwashing is all about. In line with the themes of the book, our focus is on what Jesus' washing of his disciples' feet reveals about the nature of power as seen through God's eyes, and hence the liturgy's political message. We argue that through the act of footwashing, Jesus shows us a radically new way to live at loggerheads with the liberal worldview.

Footwashing—social and liturgical

It is widely accepted that footwashing was a common social practice in Jesus' day. Thomas O'Loughlin, seeking to illustrate just how common, describes it as being as ubiquitous as brushing your teeth!* However, there's a difference. Footwashing, unlike brushing one's teeth, was firmly implicated in the social hierarchy of Jesus' day. That is, hosts would invite their guests to have their feet washed, but since this was regarded as a menial task, it was typically carried out by someone of low social status like a slave, and often a woman.

Today, *Common Worship* allows for the practice of the washing of feet in Holy Week, set within the larger Liturgy of Maundy Thursday. The service incorporates a Eucharist and includes The Stripping of the Sanctuary

---

* Thomas O'Loughlin, *Washing Feet: Imitating the Example of Jesus in the Liturgy Today* (Collegeville, MN: Liturgical Press, 2015), p. 32.

in preparation for Good Friday, followed by The Watch, when in darkness we are invited to remember Jesus in the Garden of Gethsemane before his arrest. John 13 is read, and there are various themed prayers, notably of a penitential nature:

> Purge us from our sin and we shall be clean;
> wash us and we shall be whiter than snow.

However, in contrast to the liturgies of Baptism or Eucharist, there's little provided in the way of elaborate or carefully crafted words to surround the act of footwashing itself. *Common Worship* suggests that the anthem *Ubi caritas* ("Where charity and love are, there God is") may be sung during the footwashing and offers a prayer to be used at the end of the symbolic act, but otherwise the rubric simply reads:

> The president may wash the feet of some members of the congregation.

It is this which has created space for the rather stylized approach to footwashing described above. That said, there are more meaningful, though undoubtedly more messy models out there, notably where everyone involved both washes and has their feet washed.*

---

* Jean Vanier, *The Scandal of Service: Jesus Washes Our Feet* (London: Darton, Longman & Todd, 1997).

To go more deeply into the meaning and significance of the act of footwashing, particularly the way in which it turns ideas of power on their head, it is necessary to delve into the fourth Gospel text from which the practice comes.

John 13—key features and what they reveal

John 13 contains a number of defining features which provide the context in which Jesus' washing of the disciples' feet takes place. Three stand out.

First, the text marks the beginning of Jesus' farewell to his disciples—Chapters 14–17 are often referred to as the "Farewell Discourse"—and from this we can conclude that footwashing is intimately linked to Jesus' passion and death. The passage from the fourth Gospel confirms this, beginning:

> Now before the festival of the Passover, Jesus knew that his hour had come to depart from this world and go to the Father.
>
> *John 13:1*

Second, and unsurprisingly given the first point, the scene is one of evident pain and anguish, but also glory.

Jesus, we are told, is "troubled in spirit" (John 13:21) as he contemplates the behaviour of his disciples and his knowledge of what is to come. This includes Peter's resistance to having his feet washed ("You will never wash my feet") and his misunderstanding as to the deeper meaning of the act ("Lord, not my feet only but also my hands and my head!"), Judas's betrayal, and Peter's bravado ("I will lay down my life for you"). There is also Jesus' knowledge that Peter will desert him in the aftermath of his arrest (John 13:38). "Do quickly what you are going to do," says Jesus to Judas as the devil enters him (John 13:27).

But notwithstanding Jesus' pain and anguish, it is also precisely at the moment when Judas goes out that Jesus speaks of glory:

> Now the Son of Man has been glorified, and
> God has been glorified in him.
>
> *John 13:31*

It is for this reason, unusually for Lent, that the Maundy Thursday liturgy includes the option to sing or say the Gloria, capturing the Christian view that betrayal and suffering (which are the focus of this rite) are the route to glory.

But there is a third defining feature of John 13 which is also worth noting. Against the backdrop of pain and anguish, resistance and betrayal, what is most striking is the tenderness and intimacy of the scene.

The footwashing occurs during the sharing of food. It involves touch (i.e. the washing and drying of feet). Jesus is partially undressed, having taken off his outer robe. Peter and the disciple "whom Jesus loved" are lying with their heads on Jesus' chest—a fact rather concealed in the NRSV translation, which prefers "reclining" to the more explicit mention of their lying or leaning on Jesus' bosom or breast, as suggested by a more direct translation from the Greek.

Furthermore, Jesus calls his disciples "little children" (John 13: 33), and he even feeds his soon-to-be betrayer, Judas, by putting a piece of dipped bread directly in his mouth (John 13:26).

It is in this context of saying goodbye, pain and anguish, tenderness and intimacy, and yet glory, that Jesus washes his disciples' feet. But what does this mean?

Power as seen through God's eyes

Jesus' act of footwashing—often resisted, often done perfunctorily in the Church—turns worldly notions of power and strength on their head as the creator of heaven and earth, the one who rules the constellations, the one before whom we should fall to our knees and worship, falls to his knees to wash the disciples' feet!*

In the words of the twelfth-century Cistercian monk Aelred of Rievaulx:

---

*   Michael Perham, *The Way of Christ-Likeness: Being Transformed by the Liturgies of Lent, Holy Week and Easter* (Norwich: Canterbury Press, 2016), pp. 61–4.

> ... consider what majesty it is that is washing
> and drying the feet of mere mortals, what
> graciousness it is that touches with his sacred
> hands the feet of the traitor. Look and wait
> and, last of all, give him your own feet to wash,
> because those whom he does not wash will have
> no part with him.*

Jesus' act of footwashing is the very opposite of our normal human response to opposition, misunderstanding, denial and betrayal, when we are often prone to anger, hurt, incomprehension, indignation and lashing out. With Jesus, there is no will to worldly power, only intimacy, vulnerability, gentleness and love. Moreover, when Peter draws his sword as the authorities come to arrest his master, Jesus again asserts the peaceable nature of his kingdom:

> Put your sword back into its sheath. Am I not
> to drink the cup that the Father has given me?
> *John 18:11*

And then before Pilate, Jesus again reiterates the non-violent nature of his rule:

---

*   Aelred of Rievaulx, "A Rule of Life for a Recluse", in *Celebrating the Seasons: Daily Spiritual Readings for the Christian Year*, compiled and introduced by Robert Atwell (Norwich: Canterbury Press, 1999), p. 212.

My kingdom is not from this world. If my
kingdom were from this world, my followers
would be fighting to keep me from being handed
over to the Jews. But as it is, my kingdom is not
from here.

John 18:36

But there's more to say. It is not just that Jesus turns
worldly ideas of hierarchy and what constitutes
strength on their head, he also gives us a new vision
of community—of how we are to be with each other—
which breaks down barriers and binds us together, and
where everyone, whoever they are, must welcome, love
and serve each other. Once again, this vision, which
draws us into the mystery of God's love, is far removed
from liberal ideas of the individuality of the human race,
where human beings need protecting from each other
to stop us interfering in each other's rights.

To conclude . . .

Jesus' actions in washing his disciples' feet are
undoubtedly shocking and scandalous, and Peter's
reaction is at one level entirely understandable. And
yet, at the same time, Peter's response reveals something
profound about the challenge of discipleship—our
discipleship. Peter—like most of us—is still wedded to
the hierarchy and violence of the world and the illusion

of self-sufficiency. The idea that his "Teacher and Lord" would wash his feet appals him. He has yet to own up to his own fragility and fearfulness, preferring the bravado of strength and being in control. And yet it is only when he comes face to face with his weakness—his dark night of the soul—that he realizes his need for Jesus' cleansing and healing touch.

I remember Larrie, a retired holistic beauty therapist and a member of our Cathedral community. She washed the feet of the homeless men at our winter night shelter. Surrounded by fairy lights and candles in the cloister just outside the Chapter House, and with attractive drapes on the wall, the guests would sit with their feet in bowls of warm, soapy water. Larrie would talk to them, and they'd open up to her as she massaged their weary feet and gave them clean socks to wear. It was beautiful and always struck me as far closer to what Jesus intended than the footwashing we did on Maundy Thursday.

For reflection or discussion

1. What does the act of footwashing as described in John 13 tell us about the nature of God?
2. How does the idea of footwashing in Christianity challenge liberal ideas of what it is to be human?
3. What can we learn from Peter's reaction to Jesus' desire to wash his feet—and how might that work out in our own discipleship journey?

4. How might footwashing be done more meaningfully in our churches?

Further reading

Thomas O'Loughlin, *Washing Feet: Imitating the Example of Jesus in the Liturgy Today* (Collegeville, MN: Liturgical Press, 2015).

Jean Vanier, *The Scandal of Service: Jesus Washes Our Feet* (London: Darton, Longman & Todd, 1997).

CHAPTER 7

Funeral

Support us, O Lord,
all the day long of this troublous life,
until the shadows lengthen and the evening comes,
the busy world is hushed,
the fever of life is over
and our work is done.
Then, Lord, in your mercy grant us a safe lodging,
a holy rest, and peace at the last;
through Christ our Lord. Amen.
A Prayer of John Henry Newman

Paul Sheppy, in his two-volume *Death Liturgy and Ritual*, makes the interesting observation that compared with past generations, who were intimate with death and dying and yet kept the funeral impersonal, we are much more remote from death but like our funerals intimate and personal. As he says, "We have simply transposed remoteness and intimacy."* The 1662 funeral service doesn't even mention the name of the deceased. Instead, reference is made rather starkly to "the corpse" or, more affectionately, to "our dear brother"—and presumably on occasions "sister"! However, there's no sermon in the 1662 service, let alone a eulogy about the life of the deceased. A sermon was introduced as an option with the *Alternative Service Book* in 1980, but it wasn't until the arrival of *Common Worship* in 2000 that provision was made for there to be tributes to the deceased as well.

It is worth reflecting on this shift—from an intimacy with death (against an impersonal funeral) to today's polar opposite where we experience remoteness from death alongside the personalization of the funeral—as it reveals much about our contemporary liberal (and no doubt post-modern) condition.

Death has become more remote because with advances in medical science, sudden and premature death has become less common, at least in places of peace and prosperity. In addition, the medicalization of death has taken death out of the home and into hospitals and hospices. Add to this the industrialization of the disposal of bodies with crematoria, gathering pace in the twentieth century, and we can further see the way in

---

*   Paul P. J. Sheppy, *Death Liturgy and Ritual Volume II: A Commentary on Liturgical Texts* (Aldershot: Ashgate, 2004), p. 33.

which death has become more remote to us.* How many of us, for instance, regularly attend open coffin wakes?

And yet it is against this backdrop of greater distance from death and industrial-style cremation that mourners have wanted to celebrate the individuality of the deceased, with some people even planning their own funeral. Favourite pieces of music, poems and special tributes by friends and family are all the norm.** In an age when we are often said to be in denial about death, and when we expect the medical profession to be able to do more and more to prevent it, it is almost as if this attention to the shape and feel of the funeral represents a last-ditch attempt at control even in the face of death. Liberal ideas of autonomy run amok, we might say!

In this chapter, we explore how Christian liturgy speaks about death (and life) in the funeral service. We are again interested in ways in which the liturgy challenges contemporary (liberal) norms. We first consider Christianity's distinctive relationship with death before looking at what is communicated in the funeral service more broadly. We argue that, through the liturgy, the Church does not duck the reality of death but reminds us that we are God's and encourages us, like Jesus, to surrender ourself to God. At the same time, the liturgy is replete with references to our rich and ongoing

---

*   Paul P. J. Sheppy, *Death Liturgy and Ritual Volume I: A Pastoral and Liturgical Theology* (Aldershot: Ashgate, 2003), pp. 3–8.

**   "Always look on the bright side of life" is one of the most popular songs requested for funerals.

relationships, even unto death. As is now a recurring theme, so much for a vision of the private liberal self!

There's one additional opening point we should make. It is well known that there is a growing gap between what the Church has said historically about death and what most people—both inside and outside the Church—believe. Without giving up on ideas of eternity, heaven and life beyond death, the challenge for the Church is to be able to articulate—for those who ask—what the (largely symbolic) language it uses refers to. This is no mean feat, and it requires openness and pastoral sensitivity. We will return to this issue at the end of the chapter, but first let us consider Christianity's particular relationship with death.

Christianity and death

As the religion which revolves around the cross, an instrument of torture and execution, Christianity has always had a distinctive relationship with death. Moreover, in the life of the Church, it is not just when someone dies that this is apparent. Rather, all the Church's liturgies are peppered with references to death—as we have seen. At our baptism, for instance, when we are reminded that our body is not our own, we are signed with the cross and symbolically "drowned" in the waters of baptism. As the Prayer over the Water in the baptism service says:

We thank you, Father, for the water of baptism.
In it we are buried with Christ in his death.

Moreover, every time we attend a Eucharist, we proclaim Christ crucified (1 Corinthians 1:23–24). As one of the Acclamations during some of the Eucharistic Prayers has it:

When we eat this bread and drink this cup,
we proclaim your death, Lord Jesus,
until you come in glory.

So why this distinctive emphasis?

Because Christians believe that in rising to new life, Jesus has won a glorious victory. As the Easter Song of Praise (the *Exsultet*), often sung on Easter Eve, puts it:

This is the night when Jesus Christ vanquished hell,
broke the chains of death
and rose triumphant from the grave.

Or as St Paul says:

"Death has been swallowed up in victory."
"Where, O death, is your victory? Where, O death, is your sting?"

1 Corinthians 15:54b–55

And this, Christians believe, has implications for us too, giving hope in death and new life in Christ even after death. Bold claims, to be sure, but claims Christianity makes nevertheless.

This, for instance, is how it is expressed in one of the short Proper Prefaces recommended for use at a funeral in the context of a Eucharist:

> And now we give you thanks
> because through him you have given us
> the hope of a glorious resurrection;
> so that, although death comes to us all,
> yet we rejoice in the promise of eternal life;
> for to your faithful people life is
>   changed, not taken away;
> and when our mortal flesh is laid aside
> an everlasting dwelling place is made
>   ready for us in heaven.

So as the liturgy puts it, at death, life is changed but not taken away, and there is a place for us in heaven (John 14:1–3). It is this focus on death as a gateway to life—and a sense in which our ultimate destiny is to be with God—which is then played out in the funeral service as the Church seeks to mark this important rite of passage both for the deceased and for those who mourn.

The funeral liturgy

Common Worship provides resources for use when someone is close to death and for before and after the funeral service. There are also orders for the funeral of a child and for a memorial service. More than this, there is rich material relating to death and the promise of life with God throughout the liturgical year, notably during Holy Week and Easter but also at All Saints and All Souls.

The funeral service, which can be held within a service of Communion, is divided into six sections: the Gathering; readings and a sermon (the Liturgy of the Word); Prayers; Commendation and Farewell (when the deceased is placed in God's care); the Committal (when the body is committed for cremation or burial); and the Dismissal, including a closing blessing.

As the coffin is received into the church or crematorium before the funeral, *Common Worship* says it may be sprinkled with water, using words recalling the baptism of the deceased:

> With this water we call to mind *N*'s [the
>   deceased's name] baptism.
> As Christ went through the deep
>   waters of death for us,
> so may he bring us to the fullness of resurrection life
> with *N* and all the redeemed.

So there is a sense that Christ has gone ahead of us and that God is no stranger to death.

The funeral service usually begins with a series of sentences from Scripture, sometimes as the coffin is brought into church, accompanied by the immediate family of the deceased. The sentences emphasize the promise of eternal life, God's faithfulness, mercy and love, and our dependence on God:

> We brought nothing into the world,
>   and we take nothing out.
> The Lord gave, and the Lord has taken away;
>   blessed be the name of the Lord.
> > *1 Timothy 6:7; Job 1:21b*

The service is then introduced with a reminder of the funeral's purpose, which is at once practical, pastoral and theological:

> We have come here today
> to remember before God our
>   *brother/sister [sibling] N*;
> to give thanks for *his/her [their]* life;
> to commend *him/her [them]* to God our
>   merciful redeemer and judge;
> to commit *his/her [their]* body to
>   be *buried/cremated*,
> and to comfort one another in our grief.*

---

* *Common Worship* does not yet include entirely gender-inclusive language. The additions in parentheses are mine.

After an opening prayer, there is an opportunity to sing (as there is again later) and for tributes to the deceased. This is followed by (optional) prayers of penitence, where we ask for God's forgiveness, and a Collect where it is prayed that those who mourn will be comforted and grow in faith.

As we come to the readings and sermon, Psalm 23 is offered as a possibility, with its customary reassurance alongside a reminder of the reality of death:

> Though I walk through the valley
>   of the shadow of death,
> I will fear no evil;
> for you are with me;
> your rod and your staff, they comfort me.
>
> *Psalm 23:4*

The sermon, which *Common Worship* indicates is designed to "proclaim the gospel in the context of the death of this particular person", is followed by prayers. These typically give thanks for the life of the deceased and pray for those who mourn, for healing where there are feelings of hurt or regret, and for those still living, that we may use our remaining time on earth in ways which honour God.

We then come to the point in the service at which the deceased is commended to God. Once again, Christ's victory over death is recalled:

God our creator and redeemer,
by your power Christ conquered death
and entered into glory.
Confident of his victory and claiming his promises,
we entrust N to your mercy
in the name of Jesus our Lord,
who died and is alive
and reigns with you,
now and for ever.

There then follows the Committal for cremation or burial, and finally the Dismissal. At the Committal, God's promises are once more emphasized, but we are also reminded of the fleeting nature of our days with words from Psalm 103:

For he knows of what we are made;
he remembers that we are but dust.
Our days are like the grass;
we flourish like a flower of the field;
when the wind goes over it, it is gone
and its place will know it no more.
But the merciful goodness of the Lord endures
for ever and ever towards those that fear him
and his righteousness upon their children's children.

So what does this add up to?

Based on the preceding analysis, a number of themes can be clearly seen. First, the funeral liturgy looks death square in the face. Death is real. It is not "nothing at all".* Secondly, the liturgy is clear about our end—as it is about our beginning—an end to which we are encouraged to surrender:

> N, go forth from this world:
> in the love of God the Father who created you . . .
> "Father, into your hands I commend my spirit."
> *Luke 23:46*

But more than this, what come across most strongly in the liturgy are the rich relationships within which both we and the deceased are embedded, even after death. As the *Common Worship* introduction to the season of All Saints says:

> No Christian is solitary. Through baptism we become members one of another in Christ, members of a company of saints whose mutual belonging transcends death.

And in the life of the Church, the living and the dead are never considered very far apart, as one of Charles Wesley's hymns expresses:

> One family we dwell in him,

---

* This alludes to the comment by Henry Scott Holland (often quoted out of context) in his sermon entitled "Death the King of Terrors", delivered following the death of King Edward VII in 1910.

> one Church above, beneath,
> though now divided by the stream,
> the narrow stream of death.

There's our own continued relationship with those we love and see no more. There's the continued relationship of the deceased with God. As the funeral liturgy expresses:

> Heavenly Father,
> you have not made us for darkness and death,
> but for life with you for ever.

There's also the relationship of the deceased with the Communion of Saints, and the faithful who have gone before us:

> Give rest, O Christ, to your servant with the saints:
> where sorrow and pain are no more,
> neither sighing but life everlasting.

Or, with baptismal and eucharistic overtones, the relationship of the deceased with the saints is expressed as follows:

> In baptism, *he/she* was *[they were]* made
>   by adoption a child of God.
> At the eucharist *he/she* was *[they*
>   *were]* sustained and fed.

> God now welcomes *him/her [them]*
>   to his table in heaven
> to share in eternal life with all the saints.

Then there is our own relationships with the saints. The liturgical material for All Saints and All Souls is again evocative, noting our closeness to the angels and saints and the way in which we follow their example, are strengthened by their fellowship, and are joined with them in prayer:

> We give you thanks
> for the whole company of your saints in glory,
> with whom in fellowship we join
>   our prayers and praises;
> by your grace may we, like them,
>   be made perfect in love.

Indeed, the relationship between us and the saints is felt to be so close that we are often addressed in the liturgy in the very same breath, looking ahead to the day when we will all be reunited in the final consummation of God's new creation in Christ. William Cavanaugh describes this moment of "communion"—a further blurring of the temporal and eternal—not as an escape from "this-worldly politics" but rather a "radical interruption of the false politics of the earthly city". In fact, he says, this uniting of heaven and earth, when everything will be seen for what it is, is the "true politics".*

What do we believe?

At the start of the chapter, I noted the growing gap between what the Church historically has said about life after death and what people actually believe. Whatever the Church says, in wider society belief in personal survival after death is somewhat threadbare. The challenge for the Church is to explain to a new generation what it is that language it uses concretely refers to. This includes being honest about what we cannot know. Vernon White, former Canon Theologian at Westminster Abbey, who pleads for the Church to keep talking about eternity, sets the task in the context of a continued sense of transcendence—of something beyond—that so many people feel, a sense that won't go away, regardless of people's attitudes to Christian doctrine. White sees this in ordinary life in our sense of order and play, in our humour and hope, and in our sense of incompleteness and longing. Of course, just because we may wish for something, doesn't make it

---

*   William Cavanaugh, "The City: Beyond secular parodies", in John Milbank, Catherine Pickstock and Graham Ward (eds), *Radical Orthodoxy: A New Theology* (London and New York: Routledge, 1999), p. 185.

true. But equally, as White points out, it doesn't make it false.*

A good place to start, as the Church of today seeks to ensure that what it says about life and death is helpful and coherent, is to ask what the language the Church uses—as expressed in our liturgies—tells us about how we understand both the nature of God and what it is to be human. After all, this is surely why the Church attempts to say anything at all!

What we then see is that for God to be God—the God who creates us, knows us and loves us—God simply cannot let us go:

> For since we believe that Jesus died and rose again, even so, through Jesus, God will bring with [God] those who have died.
>
> *1 Thessalonians 4:14*

As the verse expresses, this is a lovely image of the God who out of love for the world sent his son to die for us, and who cannot but bring us with him! So, much of what is expressed in the liturgy is trying to be true to our convictions about God.

Second, that the Church has said historically that those who die need to "wait" until the resurrection on the last day, may be because of a sense of what it is to be human. Our humanity is found in our relationships with

---

*   Vernon White, *Life Beyond Death: Threads of Hope in Faith, Life and Theology* (London: Darton, Longman & Todd, 2006).

God and each other. As is emphasized again and again in the Church's liturgy, we make no sense except in and through our relationships. Thus we can't be redeemed on our own. We have to wait! Equally, language about bodily resurrection doesn't need to be understood woodenly, but more in terms of what it says about being human. We are not simply spirit and never can be!

Conclusion

If in contemporary society we are remote from death, compared to our forebears, but like our funerals to express our individuality and our autonomy, the funeral liturgy seeks to remind us of our mortality, of whose we are, encouraging us—like Jesus—to surrender our self to God in whom we have our beginning and end. It is in this context that harking back to our baptism at our funeral makes sense. All this is profoundly counter-cultural: the liberal self isn't inclined to surrender itself to anyone! At the same time, the liturgy is acutely focused on our relationality, not our individuality—in life and in death—and for God's Church the living and the dead are never very far apart.

For reflection or discussion

1. Paul Sheppy says that, compared with past generations, we have simply swapped remoteness and intimacy. What does he mean, and do you agree with him?
2. What is a funeral for?
3. Christianity speaks of hope in death and new life in Christ even after death. What does the language of the funeral liturgy tell us about its understanding of God and being human?
4. In what way is the funeral liturgy political?

Further reading

Janet Morley, *Our Last Awakening: Poems for Living in the Face of Death* (London: SPCK, 2016).

Vernon White, *Life Beyond Death: Threads of Hope in Faith, Life and Theology* (London: Darton, Longman & Todd, 2006).

Conclusion

When they had finished breakfast, Jesus said to Simon Peter, "Simon son of John, do you love me more than these?" He said to him, "Yes, Lord; you know that I love you." Jesus said to him, "Feed my lambs." A second time he said to him, "Simon son of John, do you love me?" He said to him, "Yes, Lord; you know that I love you." Jesus said to him, "Tend my sheep." He said to him the third time, "Simon son of John, do you love me?" Peter felt hurt because he said to him the third time, "Do you love me?" And he said to him, "Lord, you know everything; you know that I love you." Jesus said to him, "Feed my sheep."

John 21:15–17

In Chapter 6, we noted Peter's horror at Jesus' suggestion that he should wash Peter's feet, arguing that Peter's resistance to having his feet washed tells us a lot about how he had yet to own up to his own fragility and fearfulness, preferring the bravado of strength and being in control.

The passage cited above—from John 21—offers a kind of denouement of this whole episode, where after Peter's denial of Jesus following Jesus' arrest, Peter is rehabilitated—asked three times by the risen Jesus whether he loves him and instructed to feed his sheep. Peter, we are told in verse 17, felt hurt that Jesus asked him three times, reminding us again of Peter's fragility and dependence even as he is brought back into the fold.

Peter's fragility and dependence—our own fragility and dependence—seems an appropriate way to start as we bring this book, ultimately about mission, to a close.

In the introduction, we noted the countless ways in which churches bring hope and the love of Jesus to communities up and down the land. And yet, at the same time, we pointed to a certain fragility or lack of confidence within the Church, sometimes partially concealed by a busy-ness and a breathlessness. Despite all this, we argued that Christianity is still electric, fresh, relevant, contemporary and radical, and hence that we can be confident in the God who is faithful!

Part of the problem, we suggested, is that we seem to have internalized the perception that the Church is not a "happening" place. We are largely unaware that our liturgies say something radical and exciting in relation to the dominant creed by which we live in Europe and North America, namely political liberalism (mainly because we are not well-versed in what liberalism says).*

---

*   The most powerful creeds are always the ones that have a hold on us without us knowing it.

In turn, we argued that the Church's liturgy is political, because it tells a radically different story about the nature of the world and our place in it from the liberal creed that dominates. Stories are always political.

At the same time, we said that this is a book about mission, expressing the hope that after reading the book, your experience of the liturgy, your sense of how the Church is political, and your confidence (just the right amount of confidence!) as missionary disciples would be transformed.

In this Conclusion, we revisit all these issues, asking what we have learnt and what the implications are for thinking about God's mission and how the Church is political. We first look at the abiding messages we can take from our exploration of the Church's liturgy in respect of political liberalism. We then consider the implications of what we have uncovered for thinking about mission before finally restating—more fulsomely, we hope—what it means to say the Church is political. The chapter necessarily operates at a level of abstraction which is different from the others, but the hope is that having digested the earlier chapters you will grasp the points being made here and be able to relate them to your own experience and practice.

The Church and political liberalism

The Church is political because through its liturgies it tells a story at odds with political liberalism, the dominant creed we live by in Europe and North America.

The Church believes in the natural unity of humanity, not our separateness as in liberalism with its partial and reductionist understanding of human beings as individuals who need protecting from each other. The Church, by contrast, argues that we are most truly ourselves in relationship with one another and with God. Indeed, it suggests we make little sense as persons apart from our relationships.

The Church, again in contrast to liberalism, believes that human beings have goods in common, notwithstanding our differences. We *can* speak in terms of ends.

The Church emphasizes not our individual autonomy or independence—like liberalism—but rather our dependence on others, and ultimately on God to whom we are encouraged to surrender, acknowledging our frailty and our neediness but also our ingenuity and creativity. Recall one of the changes that occurs in prayer, namely that our capacity to act is "preserved in its nobility" as we realize that the creator of the universe is concerned with us.*

---

*　　Peter Ochs, "Morning Prayer as Redemptive Thinking", in Randi Rashkover and C.C. Pecknold (eds), *Liturgy, Time, and the Politics*

Moreover, the Church doesn't regard individual freedom (negative freedom) as a good or an end in and of itself—like liberalism—preferring instead to emphasize how we need to be formed in community in order to be able to make life-giving choices.

In Chapters 3 to 7, we saw all these things emphasized repeatedly in the liturgy: in the Eucharist with its emphasis on recovering our natural unity in Christ, in the richness of the diverse relationships in which we are embedded in life and in death, and in baptism when, as Frederick Bauerschmidt reminds us, the illusion of control is the chief spirit which needs casting out.*

None of this delivers for us a "how-to guide" regarding a Christian position on every issue, but it does give us some fundamental post-liberal principles to guide our thinking and our acting. The whole question of human rights (individual rights), for instance, at least looks different from the perspective of Christian liturgy.**

But what about mission?

---

of Redemption (Grand Rapids, MI: William B. Eerdmans Publishing Company and London: SCM Press, 2006), p. 85.

* Frederick Christian Bauerschmidt, "Being Baptized: Bodies and Abortion", in Stanley Hauerwas and Samuel Wells (eds), *The Blackwell Companion to Christian Ethics*, 2nd edn (Malden, MA, Oxford and Carlton Victoria: Blackwell Publishing, 2011), p. 256.

** Rowan Williams, "Do human rights exist?" and "Reconnecting human rights and religious faith" in Rowan Williams, *Faith in the Public Square* (London: Bloomsbury, 2012), pp. 149–72.

The Church and mission

The book's focus on the Church's liturgy, and how it tells a story profoundly at odds with political liberalism, while an end in itself was also a means to an end, namely to gain clarity and confidence in relation to mission.

But to adopt such an approach—i.e. to focus on what Christianity says *distinctively* through its liturgy—is already, potentially, to take a position on mission. One of the big divides in the Church when thinking about mission is between those who emphasize Christianity's distinctiveness and those who emphasize the importance of dialogue. That is, for some, Christianity says some particular things which are (fairly) non-negotiable while, for others, what Christianity says is revealed afresh in specific times and places, always necessitating the need for dialogue.* In focusing on the Church's liturgy, this book might be seen as putting distinctiveness before dialogue. But this is not the case. Yes, Christianity says some particular things, which we have seen throughout the book, but the truth is always discerned in dialogue even if the institutional church often struggles with this.

Some of the most exciting approaches to mission seek to steer a path through the distinctiveness/dialogue maze: indeed, arguing that both approaches need each other.** Andrew Shanks, for instance, speaks of the

---

* Malcom Brown, *Tensions in Christian Ethics: An Introduction* (London: SPCK, 2010), pp. 14–19.

** Ibid., p.134.

importance of both the "virtue of sanctity" (i.e. paying attention to what Christianity says distinctively) and the "virtue of transgression" (i.e. crossing boundaries between Christian and other cultures to interpret each to the other as effectively as possible).* Echoing Rowan Williams, Anna Rowlands talks about an approach to mission which can recognize and honour difference, is able to contemplate dispossession of narrow practices of self-assertion—*not my will but yours be done* (Luke 22:42)—and then is committed to negotiate goods in common (i.e. recognition, dispossession, negotiation).** That is, the Church should not become just another interest group clamouring for its rights. And lastly, Al Barrett is pushing in a similar direction when he suggests that the Church needs to shift its imagination "towards expecting to discover abundance not primarily in [its] liturgical 'centres', but at and beyond the 'edges' of church", including "receiving 'communion' at 'tables' and 'places' that are far from our own 'ecclesial' centres".*** Distinctiveness and dialogue, therefore: the two must be married.

---

*   Andrew Shanks, *Civil Society, Civil Religion* (Oxford: Blackwell, 1995), p. 11.

**   Anna Rowlands, "Fraternal Traditions: Anglican Social Theology and Catholic Social Teaching in a British Context", in Malcolm Brown (ed.), *Anglican Social Theology: Renewing the Vision Today* (London: Church House Publishing, 2014), pp. 160–5.

*** Al Barrett, *Interrupting the Church's Flow: Developing a radically receptive political theology in the urban margins* (London: SCM Press, 2020), pp. 11–12.

There is a second key issue at stake when we think about mission, and that is about the will to power. In one breath, we might say that as Christianity's colonial past has receded into history—formally if not always temperamentally—there is greater recognition that mission is about encounter and embrace.* But in reality, the tendency towards mission as the will to power is never very far away. It is here that Peter's story—his dark night of the soul (from which he comes back)—or Williams' point about mission as "dispossession" becomes important. That is, any reflection on mission must begin with ourselves in order that we don't, on account of our own inadequacies, end up lording it over others. Or, as Barrett asks, how might the "other" have positive agency of their own as we engage in mission?** Christianity has not historically been very good at this, but it is a key question as we consider the Church's approach to mission. It is of great concern when mission strategies are devised far from those places or communities that society marginalizes, as the danger is that local people won't have agency and that power imbalances are maintained.***

And what about this book's argument that the Church is political?

---

*   Ibid., pp. 23–4.

** Ibid., p. 25.

*** Mike Pears and Paul Cloke (eds), *Mission in Marginal Places: The Theory* (Milton Keynes: Paternoster, 2016).

The Church and politics

The Church is political, we have said, because it tells a story through its liturgies about the nature of the world, and our place in it, at odds with the political liberal creed which predominates. However, in the Church (and in wider society), we find the notion that our liturgy is political hard to comprehend. Indeed, we frequently resist it!

But what the argument that the Church is political means, if we take it to its logical conclusion, is that if we want to influence, say, the Prime Minister on any given issue we should invite them to a service of Holy Communion (leaving aside for a moment whether they would come!).

But if this notion seems strange to us—we'd far rather lobby the Prime Minister or launch a campaign—it is evidence, again, that we struggle to grasp how the Church is political in the sense argued in this book.

The danger when we lobby a politician or launch a campaign is that we conceive of the Church as only *indirectly* political (i.e. seeking to persuade the government, which we view as the "true" arbiter of politics, to pursue this or that action). Moreover, to view the Church's political role like this is often to limit it to engaging in politics on politically liberal terms. And yet Christianity, as we have seen throughout this book, rejects this vision.

So to say that the Church—a space cleared in the universe where we can see clearly—is political is to say that it is a political space in its own right. Moreover, the Church as a directly political body is not to be found in political liberalism, or the endless conflict between self-interested individuals, but in Christ where all people are gathered together in God's kingdom "to feast with all the saints" and "where the new creation is brought to perfection". As the Eucharistic Liturgy puts it, this is our end.

Therefore, it is not so much that the Church *acts upon* the state or government as the place where politics "truly happens", but rather that the state—all human affairs—sits within the Christian story. Thus the Church and the state *share* the social and political space *for the sake of God's mission*.*

None of this is to reject the reality of our world and its forms of governance (though theologically speaking they have a provisional quality to them). Christians will rightly lobby and engage in campaigns, and it is perfectly possible that the work of government, or anyone else, may be caught up in the saving power of God.** But to speak like this is to be clearer about the precise way in which the Church is political, and to know that the role of the Church is not to prop up the political liberal

---

*   Daniel M. Bell, Jr, "State and Civil Society", in Peter Scott and William
        T. Cavanaugh (eds), *The Blackwell Companion to Political Theology*
        (Malden, MA and Oxford: Blackwell Publishing, 2004), pp. 423–38.

**   Rowlands, "Fraternal Traditions", p. 164.

order, even while it is committed for the good of God's mission to deep and open engagement with the world in all its difference.

Finally, there is no getting away from the fact that the Church is political, which will be disappointing for some, but the way in which the Church is political, as outlined above, and explored throughout this book, should help us rise above shallow political bipartisanship and enable us to shape our lobbying and campaigning in ways which remain true to what Christianity actually believes.

For reflection or discussion

1. When you are next in church, what will you listen for in the liturgy?
2. How should your church navigate a path through the distinctiveness/dialogue maze and guard against the will to power in mission?
3. What does it mean to say the Church is a directly political body? Why is this important?
4. How might the Church's rejection of political liberalism inform your engagement in key issues of our day?

Further reading

Al Barrett and Ruth Harley, *Being Interrupted: Re-imagining the Church's Mission from the Outside In* (London: SCM Press, 2020).

Benjamin Myers, "Mission", in Benjamin Myers, *Christ the Stranger: The Theology of Rowan Williams* (London and New York: T&T Clark International, 2012), pp. 59–66.

Adrian Pabst, *Postliberal Politics: The Coming Era of Renewal* (Cambridge and Medford, MA: Polity Press, 2021).

Rowan Williams, *Being Human: Bodies, Minds, Persons* (Grand Rapids, MI: Eerdmans, 2018).

Norman Wirzba, *This Sacred Life: Humanity's Place in a Wounded World* (Cambridge: Cambridge University Press, 2021).